Rumble,
BOOM!

BY JANE BUXTON

ILLUSTRATED BY DEBE MANSFIELD

**LEARNING
MEDIA®**

The water is hot.

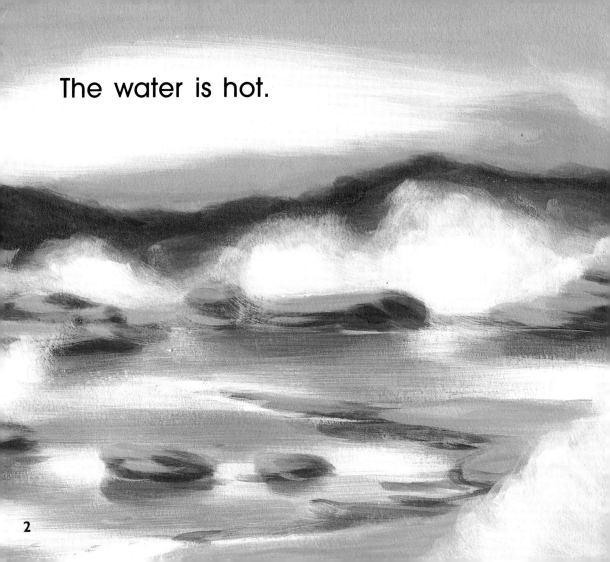

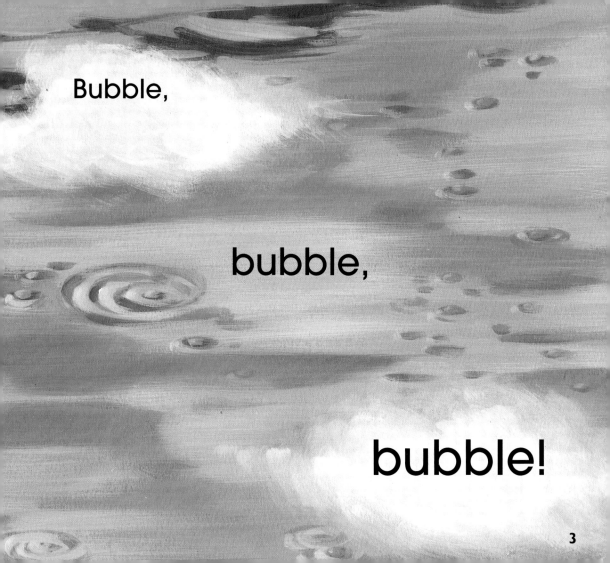

Bubble,

bubble,

bubble!

3

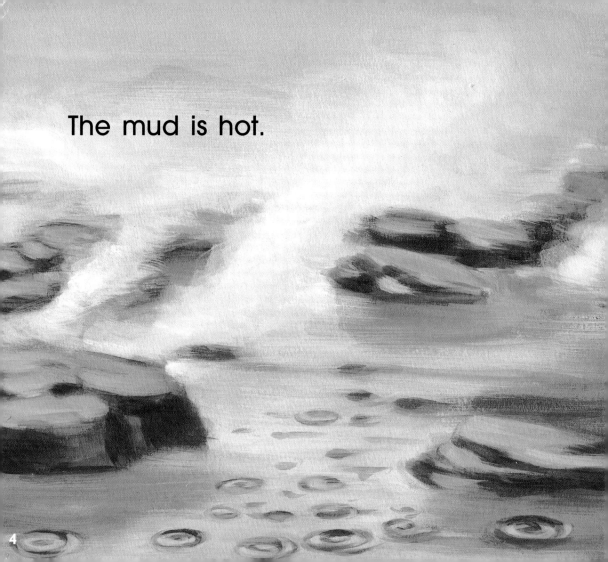

The mud is hot.

4

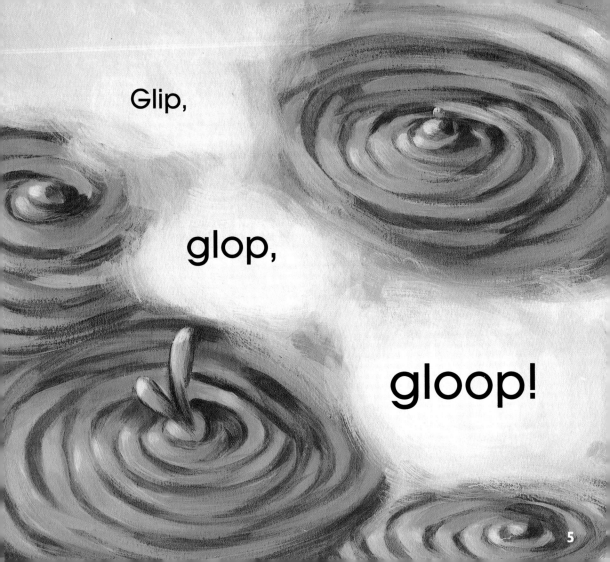

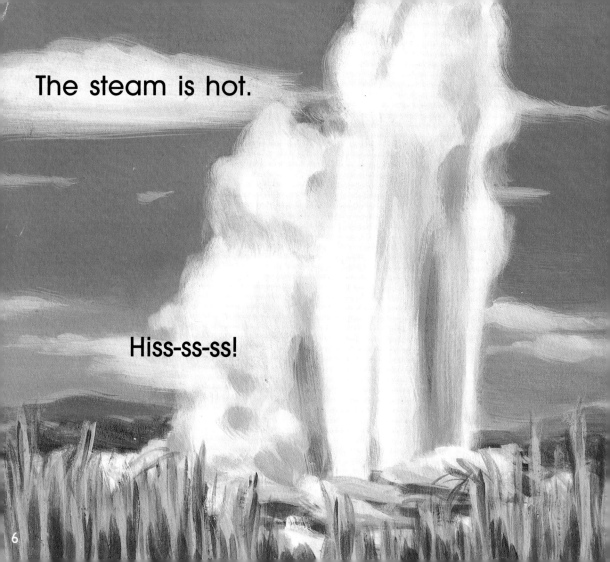

The steam is hot.

Hiss-ss-ss!

6

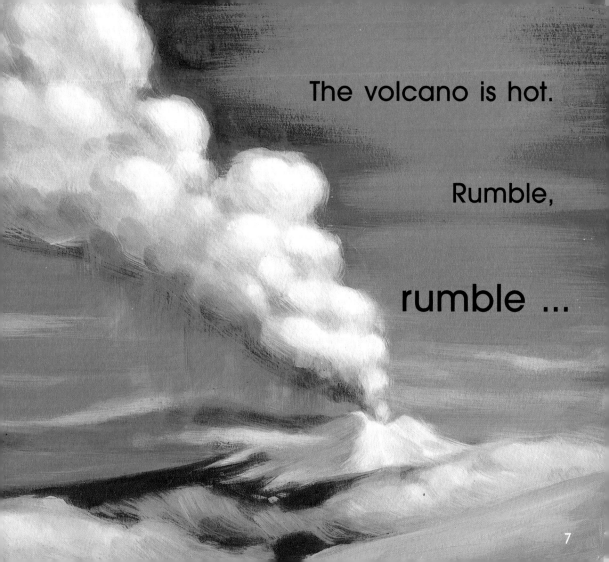

The volcano is hot.

Rumble,

rumble ...

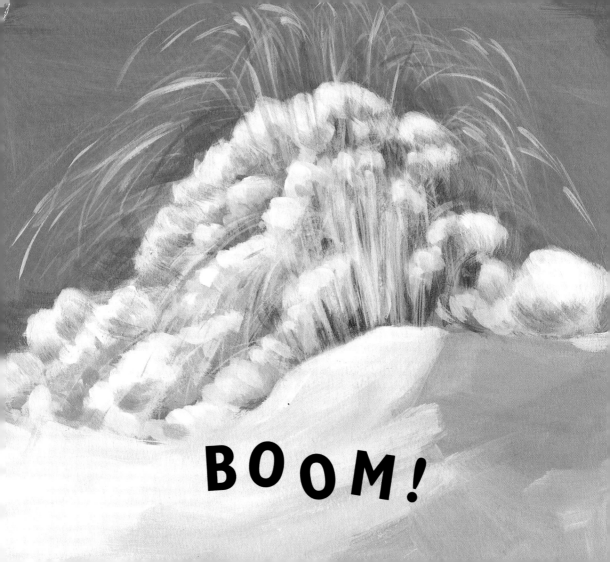